The Constitution of
The State of New Jersey:
A Quick Reference Guide

Bootblack Budget Books
Copyright 2018 ©
ISBN-13: 978-1719274623
ISBN-10: 1719274622

Contents:

Preamble – Page 3

Article I: Rights and Privileges – Page 4

Article II: Elections and Suffrage – Page 9

Article III: Distribution of the Powers of Government – Page 15

Article IV: Legislative – Page 16

Article V: Executive – Page 31

Article VI: Judicial – Page 43

Article VII: Public Officers and Employees – Page 50

Article VIII: Taxation and Finance – Page 53

Article IX: Amendments – Page 57

Article X: General Provisions – Page 59

Article XI: Schedule – Page 60

Delegates – Page 68

Preamble

We, the people of the State of New Jersey, grateful to Almighty God for the civil and religious liberty which He hath so long permitted us to enjoy, and looking to Him for a blessing upon our endeavors to secure and transmit the same unimpaired to succeeding generations, do ordain and establish this Constitution.

ARTICLE I: RIGHTS AND PRIVILEGES

Paragraph 1. All persons are by nature free and independent, and have certain natural and unalienable rights, among which are those of enjoying and defending life and liberty, of acquiring, possessing, and protecting property, and of pursuing and obtaining safety and happiness.

Paragraph 2.

(a) All political power is inherent in the people. Government is instituted for the protection, security, and benefit of the people, and they have the right at all times to alter or reform the same, whenever the public good may require it.

(b) The people reserve unto themselves the power to recall, after at least one year of service, any elected official in this State or representing this State in the United States Congress. The Legislature shall enact laws to provide for such recall elections. Any such laws shall include a provision that a recall election shall be held upon petition of at least 25% of the registered voters in the electoral district of the official sought to be recalled. If legislation to implement this constitutional amendment is not enacted within one year of the adoption of the amendment, the Secretary of State shall, by regulation, implement the constitutional amendment, except that regulations adopted by the Secretary of State shall be superseded by any subsequent legislation consistent with this constitutional amendment governing recall elections. The sufficiency of any statement of reasons or grounds procedurally required shall be a political rather than a judicial question.

Paragraph 3. No person shall be deprived of the inestimable privilege of worshipping Almighty God in a manner agreeable to the dictates of his own conscience; nor under any pretense whatever be compelled to attend any place of worship contrary to his faith and judgment; nor shall any person be obliged to pay tithes, taxes, or other rates for building or repairing any church or churches, place or places of worship, or for the maintenance of any minister or ministry, contrary to what he believes to be right or has deliberately and voluntarily engaged to perform.

Paragraph 4. There shall be no establishment of one religious sect in preference to another; no religious or racial test shall be required as a qualification for any office or public trust.

Paragraph 5. No person shall be denied the enjoyment of any civil or military right, nor be discriminated against in the exercise of any civil or military right, nor be segregated in the militia or in the public schools, because of religious principles, race, color, ancestry or national origin.

Paragraph 6. Every person may freely speak, write and publish his sentiments on all subjects, being responsible for the abuse of that right. No law shall be passed to restrain or abridge the liberty of speech or of the press. In all prosecutions or indictments for libel, the truth may be given in evidence to the jury; and if it shall appear to the jury that the matter charged as libelous is true, and was published with good motives and for justifiable ends, the party shall be acquitted; and the jury shall have the right to determine the law and the fact.

Paragraph 7. The right of the people to be secure in their persons, houses, papers, and effects, against unreasonable searches and seizures, shall not be violated; and no warrant shall issue except upon probable cause, supported by oath or affirmation, and particularly describing the place to be searched and the papers and things to be seized.

Paragraph 8. No person shall be held to answer for a criminal offense, unless on the presentment or indictment of a grand jury, except in cases of impeachment, or in cases now prosecuted without indictment, or arising in the army or navy or in the militia, when in actual service in time of war or public danger.

Paragraph 9. The right of trial by jury shall remain inviolate; but the Legislature may authorize the trial of civil causes by a jury of six persons when the matter in dispute does not exceed fifty dollars. The Legislature may provide that in any civil cause a verdict may be rendered by not less than five-sixths of the jury. The Legislature may authorize the trial of the issue of mental incompetency without a jury.

Paragraph 10. In all criminal prosecutions the accused shall have the right to a speedy and public trial by an impartial jury; to be informed of the nature and cause of the accusation; to be confronted with the witnesses against him; to have compulsory process for obtaining witnesses in his favor; and to have the assistance of counsel in his defense.

Paragraph 11. No person shall, after acquittal, be tried for the same offense. All persons shall, before conviction, be bailable by sufficient sureties, except for capital offenses when the proof is evident or presumption great.

Paragraph 12. Excessive bail shall not be required, excessive fines shall not be imposed, and cruel and unusual punishments shall not be inflicted.

Paragraph 13. No person shall be imprisoned for debt in any action, or on any judgement found upon contract, unless in cases of fraud; nor shall any person be imprisoned for a militia fine in time of peace.

Paragraph 14. The privilege of the writ of habeas corpus shall not be suspended, unless in case of rebellion or invasion the public safety may require it.

Paragraph 15. The military shall be in strict subordination to the civil power.

Paragraph 16. No soldier shall, in time of peace, be quartered in any house, without the consent of the owner; nor in time of war, except in a manner prescribed by law.

Paragraph 17. Treason against the State shall consist only in levying war against it, or in adhering to its enemies, giving them aid and comfort. No person shall be convicted of treason, unless on the testimony of two witnesses to the same overt act, or on confession in open court.

Paragraph 18. The people have the right freely to assemble together, to consult for the common good, to make known their opinions to their representatives, and to petition for redress of grievances.

Paragraph 19. Persons in private employment shall have the right to organize and bargain collectively. Persons in public employment shall have the right to organize, present to and make known to the State, or any of its political sub-divisions or agencies, their grievances and proposals through representatives of their own choosing.

Paragraph 20. Private property shall not be taken for public use without just compensation. Individuals or private corporations shall not be authorized to take private property for public use without just compensation first made to the owners.

Paragraph 21. This enumeration of rights and privileges shall not be construed to impair or deny others retained by the people.

Paragraph 22. A victim of a crime shall be treated with fairness, compassion and respect by the criminal justice system. A victim of a crime shall not be denied the right to be present at public judicial proceedings except when, prior to completing testimony as a witness, the victim is properly sequestered in accordance with law or the Rules Governing the Courts of the State of New Jersey. A victim of a crime shall be entitled to those rights and remedies as may be provided by the Legislature. For the purposes of this paragraph, "victim of a crime" means: a) a person who has suffered physical or psychological injury or has incurred loss of or damage to personal or real property as a result of a crime or an incident involving another person operating a motor vehicle while under the influence of drugs or alcohol, and b) the spouse, parent, legal guardian, grandparent, child or sibling of the decedent in the case of a criminal homicide.

Paragraph 23. 23. Every employer shall, beginning the January 1 next following the date of the approval of this amendment by the people pursuant to Article IX of the Constitution, pay each employee subject to the "New Jersey State Wage and Hour Law," P.L.1966, c.113 (C.34:11-56a et seq.), or a successor State statute, a wage rate of not less than the rate required by that act, or $8.25 per hour, whichever is more. On the September 30 next following the date of the approval of this amendment, and on September 30 of each subsequent year, the State minimum wage rate shall be increased, effective the following January 1, by any increase during the one year prior to that September 30 in the consumer price index for all urban wage earners and clerical workers (CPI-W) as calculated by the federal government. If, at any time, the federal minimum hourly wage rate set by section 6 of the federal "Fair Labor Standards Act of 1938" (29 U.S.C. s.206), or a successor federal law, is raised to a level higher than the State minimum wage rate, then the State minimum wage rate shall be increased to the level of the federal minimum wage rate and all subsequent increases based on increases in the CPI-W pursuant to this paragraph shall be applied to the State minimum wage rate as increased to match the federal minimum wage rate. This paragraph shall not be construed as altering or amending any provision of the "New Jersey State Wage and Hour Law," P.L.1966, c.113 (C.34:11-56a et seq.) or a successor State statute, other than the hourly rate set by that act, or prohibiting the Legislature from amending that act.

ARTICLE II: ELECTIONS AND SUFFRAGE

Section 1.

Paragraph 1. General elections shall be held annually on the first Tuesday after the first Monday in November; but the time of holding such elections may be altered by law. The Governor and members of the Legislature shall be chosen at general elections. Local elective officers shall be chosen at general elections or at such other times as shall be provided by law.

Paragraph 2. All questions submitted to the people of the entire State shall be voted upon at general elections.

Paragraph 3.

(a) Every citizen of the United States, of the age of 18 years, who shall have been a resident of this State and of the county in which he claims his vote 30 days, next before the election, shall be entitled to vote for all officers that now are or hereafter may be elective by the people, and upon all questions which may be submitted to a vote of the people; and

(b) Deleted by amendment.

(c) Any person registered as a voter in any election district of this State who has removed or shall remove to another state or to another county within this State and is not able there to qualify to vote by reason of an insufficient period of residence in such state or county, shall, as a citizen of the United States, have the right to vote for electors for President and Vice President of the United States, only, by Presidential Elector Absentee Ballot, in the county from which he has removed, in such manner as the Legislature shall provide.

Paragraph 4. In time of war no elector in the military service of the State or in the armed forces of the United States shall be deprived of his vote by reason of absence from his election district. The Legislature may provide for absentee voting by members of the armed forces of the United States in time of peace. The Legislature may provide the manner in which and the time and place at which such absent electors may vote, and for the return and canvass of their votes in the election district in which they respectively reside.

Paragraph 5. No person in the military, naval or marine service of the United States shall be considered a resident of this State by being stationed in any garrison, barrack, or military or naval place or station within this State.

Paragraph 6. No idiot or insane person shall enjoy the right of suffrage.

Paragraph 7. The Legislature may pass laws to deprive persons of the right of suffrage who shall be convicted of such crimes as it may designate. Any person so deprived, when pardoned or otherwise restored by law to the right of suffrage, shall again enjoy that right.

Section II.

Paragraph 1.

(a) After each federal census taken in a year ending in zero, the congressional districts shall be established by the New Jersey Redistricting Commission.
The commission shall consist of 13 members, none of whom shall be a member or employee of the Congress of the United States. The members of the commission shall be appointed with due consideration to geographic, ethnic and racial diversity and in the manner provided herein.

(b) There shall first be appointed 12 members as follows:

(1) two members to be appointed by the President of the Senate;

(2) two members to be appointed by the Speaker of the General Assembly;

(3) two members to be appointed by the minority leader of the Senate;

(4) two members to be appointed by the minority leader of the General Assembly; and

(5) four members, two to be appointed by the chairman of the State committee of the political party whose candidate for the office of Governor received the largest number of votes at the most recent gubernatorial election and two to be appointed by the chairman of the State committee of the political party whose candidate for the office of Governor received the next largest number of votes in that election.

Appointments to the commission under this subparagraph shall be made on or before June 15 of each year ending in one and shall be certified by the respective appointing officials to the Secretary of State on or before July 1 of that year. Each partisan delegation so appointed shall appoint one of its members as its chairman who shall have authority to make such certifications and to perform such other tasks as the members of that delegation shall reasonably require.

(c) There shall then be appointed one member, to serve as an independent member, who shall have been for the preceding five years a resident of this State, but who shall not during that period have held public or party office in this State. The independent member shall be appointed upon the vote of at least seven of the previously appointed members of the commission on or before July 15 of each year ending in one, and those members shall certify that appointment to the Secretary of State on or before July 20 of that year. If the previously appointed members are unable to appoint an independent member within the time allowed therefore, they shall so certify to the Supreme Court not later than that July 20 and shall include in that certification the names of the two persons who, in the members' final vote upon the appointment of the independent member, received the greatest number of votes. Not later than August 10 following receipt of that certification, the Supreme Court shall by majority vote of its full authorized membership select, of the two persons so named, the one more qualified by education and occupational experience, by prior public service in government or otherwise, and by demonstrated ability to represent the best interest of the people of this State, to be the independent member. The Court shall certify that selection to the Secretary of State not later than the following August 15.

(d) Vacancies in the membership of the commission occurring prior to the certification by the commission of Congressional districts or during any period in which the districts established by the commission may be or are under challenge in court shall be filled in the same manner as the original appointments were made within five days of their occurrence. In the case of a vacancy in the membership of the independent member, if the other members of the commission are unable to fill that vacancy within that five-day period, they shall transmit certification of such inability within three days of the expiration of the period to the Supreme Court, which shall select the person to fill the vacancy within five days of receipt of that certification.

Paragraph 2. The independent member shall serve as the chairman of the commission. The commission shall meet to organize as soon as may be practicable after certification of the appointment of the independent member, but not later than the Wednesday after the first Monday in September of each year ending in one. At the organizational meeting the members of the commission shall determine such organizational matters as they deem appropriate. Thereafter, a meeting of the commission may be called by the chairman or upon the request of seven members, and seven members of the commission shall constitute a quorum at any meeting thereof for the purpose of taking any action.

Paragraph 3. On or before the third Tuesday of each year ending in two, or within three months after receipt in each decade by the appropriate State officer of the official statement by the Clerk of the United States House of Representatives, issued pursuant to federal law, regarding the number of members of the House of Representatives apportioned to this State for that decade, whichever is later, the commission shall certify the establishment of the congressional districts to the Secretary of State. The commission shall certify the establishment of districts pursuant to a majority vote of the full authorized membership of the commission convened in open public meeting, of which meeting there shall be at least 24 hours' public notice. Any vote by the commission upon a proposal to certify the establishment of a Congressional district plan shall be taken by roll call and shall be recorded, and the vote of any member in favor of any Congressional district plan shall nullify any vote which that member shall previously have cast during the life of the commission in favor of a different Congressional district plan. If the commission is unable to certify the establishment of districts by the time required due to the inability of a plan to achieve seven votes, the two district plans receiving the greatest number of votes, but not fewer than five votes, shall be submitted to the Supreme Court, which shall select and certify whichever of the two plans so submitted conforms most closely to the requirements of the Constitution and laws of the United States.

Paragraph 4. The New Jersey Redistricting Commission shall hold at least three public hearings in different parts of the State. The commission shall, subject to the constraints of time and convenience, review written plans for the establishment of Congressional districts submitted by members of the public.

Paragraph 5. Meetings of the New Jersey Redistricting Commission shall be held at convenient times and locations and, with the exception of the public hearings required by paragraph 4 of this section and the meeting at which the establishment of districts is certified as prescribed by paragraph 3 of this section, may be closed to the public.

Paragraph 6. The Legislature shall appropriate the funds necessary for the efficient operation of the New Jersey Redistricting Commission.

Paragraph 7. Notwithstanding any provision to the contrary of this Constitution and except as otherwise required by the Constitution or laws of the United States, no court of this State other than the Supreme Court shall have jurisdiction over any judicial proceeding challenging the appointment of members to the New Jersey Redistricting Commission, or any action, including the establishment of Congressional districts, by the commission or other public officer or body under the provisions of this section.

Paragraph 8. The establishment of Congressional districts shall be used thereafter for the election of members of the House of Representatives and shall remain unaltered through the next year ending in zero in which a federal census for this State is taken.

Paragraph 9. If a plan certified by the commission is declared unlawful, the commission shall reorganize and adopt another Congressional district plan in the same manner as herein required and within the period of time prescribed by the court or within such shorter period as may be necessary to ensure that the new plan is effective for the next succeeding primary and general election for all members of the United States House of Representatives.

ARTICLE III: DISTRIBUTION OF THE POWERS OF GOVERNMENT

Paragraph 1. The powers of the government shall be divided among three distinct branches, the legislative, executive, and judicial. No person or persons belonging to or constituting one branch shall exercise any of the powers properly belonging to either of the others, except as expressly provided in this Constitution.

ARTICLE IV: LEGISLATIVE

Section I.

Paragraph 1. The legislative power shall be vested in a Senate and General Assembly.

Paragraph 2. No person shall be a member of the Senate who shall not have attained the age of thirty years, and have been a citizen and resident of the State for four years, and of the district for which he shall be elected one year, next before his election. No person shall be a member of the General Assembly who shall not have attained the age of twenty-one years and have been a citizen and resident of the State for two years, and of the district for which he shall be elected one year, next before his election. No person shall be eligible for membership in the Legislature unless he be entitled to the right of suffrage.

Paragraph 3. Each Legislature shall be constituted for a term of 2 years beginning at noon on the second Tuesday in January in each even numbered year, at which time the Senate and General Assembly shall meet and organize separately and the first annual session of the Legislature shall commence. Said first annual session shall terminate at noon on the second Tuesday in January next following, at which time the second annual session shall commence and it shall terminate at noon on the second Tuesday in January then next following but either session may be sooner terminated by adjournment sine die. All business before either House or any of the committees thereof at the end of the first annual session may be resumed in the second annual session. The legislative year shall commence at noon on the second Tuesday in January of each year.

Paragraph 4. Special sessions of the Legislature shall be called by the Governor upon petition of a majority of all the members of each house, and may be called by the Governor whenever in his opinion the public interest shall require.

Section II.

Paragraph 1. The Senate shall be composed of forty senators apportioned among Senate districts as nearly as may be according to the number of their inhabitants as reported in the last preceding decennial census of the United States and according to the method of equal proportions. Each Senate district shall be composed, wherever practicable, of one single county, and, if not so practicable, of two or more contiguous whole counties.

Paragraph 2. Each senator shall be elected by the legally qualified voters of the Senate district, except that if the Senate district is composed of two or more counties and two senators are apportioned to the district, one senator shall be elected by the legally qualified voters of each Assembly district. Each senator shall be elected for a term beginning at noon of the second Tuesday in January next following his election and ending at noon of the second Tuesday in January four years thereafter, except that each senator, to be elected for a term beginning in January of the second year following the year in which a decennial census of the United States is taken, shall be elected for a term of two years.

Paragraph 3. The General Assembly shall be composed of eighty members. Each Senate district to which only one senator is apportioned shall constitute an Assembly district. Each of the remaining Senate districts shall be divided into Assembly districts equal in number to the number of senators apportioned to the Senate district. The Assembly districts shall be composed of contiguous territory, as nearly compact and equal in the number of their inhabitants as possible, and in no event shall each such district contain less than eighty per cent nor more than one hundred twenty per cent of one-fortieth of the total number of inhabitants of the State as reported in the last preceding decennial census of the United States. Unless necessary to meet the foregoing requirements, no county or municipality shall be divided among Assembly districts unless it shall contain more than one-fortieth of the total number of inhabitants of the State, and no county or municipality shall be divided among a number of Assembly districts larger than one plus the whole number obtained by dividing the number of inhabitants in the county or municipality by one-fortieth of the total number of inhabitants of the State.

Paragraph 4. Two members of the General Assembly shall be elected by the legally qualified voters of each Assembly district for terms beginning at noon of the second Tuesday in January next following their election and ending at noon of the second Tuesday in January two years thereafter.

Section III.

Paragraph 1. After the next and every subsequent decennial census of the United States, the Senate districts and Assembly districts shall be established, and the senators and members of the General Assembly shall be apportioned among them, by an Apportionment Commission consisting of ten members, five to be appointed by the chairman of the State committee of each of the two political parties whose candidates for Governor receive the largest number of votes at the most recent gubernatorial election. Each State chairman, in making such appointments, shall give due consideration to the representation of the various geographical areas of the State. Appointments to the Commission shall be made on or before November 15 of the year in which such census is taken and shall be certified by the Secretary of State on or before December 1 of that year. The Commission, by a majority of the whole number of its members, shall certify the establishment of Senate and Assembly districts and the apportionment of senators and members of the General Assembly to the Secretary of State within one month of the receipt by the Governor of the official decennial census of the United States for New Jersey, or on or before February 1 of the year following the year in which the census is taken, whichever date is later.

Paragraph 2. If the Apportionment Commission fails so to certify such establishment and apportionment to the Secretary of State on or before the date fixed or if prior thereto it determines that it will be unable so to do, it shall so certify to the Chief Justice of the Supreme Court of New Jersey and he shall appoint an eleventh member of the Commission. The Commission so constituted, by a majority of the whole number of its members, shall, within one month after the appointment of such eleventh member, certify to the Secretary of State the establishment of Senate and Assembly districts and the apportionment of senators and members of the General Assembly.

Paragraph 3. Such establishment and apportionment shall be used thereafter for the election of members of the Legislature and shall remain unaltered until the following decennial census of the United States for New Jersey shall have been received by the Governor.

Section IV.

Paragraph 1. Any vacancy in the Legislature occasioned otherwise than by expiration of term shall be filled by election for the unexpired term only at the next general election occurring not less than 51 days after the occurrence of the vacancy, except that no vacancy shall be filled at the general election which immediately precedes the expiration of the term in which the vacancy occurs. For the interim period pending the election and qualification of a successor to fill the vacancy, or for the remainder of the term in the case of a vacancy occurring which cannot be filled pursuant to the terms of this paragraph at a general election, the vacancy shall be filled within 35 days by the members of the county committee of the political party of which the incumbent was the nominee from the municipalities or districts or units thereof which comprise the legislative district.

Paragraph 2. Each house shall be the judge of the elections, returns and qualifications of its own members, and a majority of all its members shall constitute a quorum to do business; but a smaller number may adjourn from day to day, and may be authorized to compel the attendance of absent members, in such manner, and under such penalties, as each house may provide.

Paragraph 3. Each house shall choose its own officers, determine the rules of its proceedings, and punish its members for disorderly behavior. It may expel a member with the concurrence of two-thirds of all its members.

Paragraph 4. Each house shall keep a journal of its proceedings, and from time to time publish the same. The yeas and nays of the members of either house on any question shall, on demand of one-fifth of those present, be entered on the journal.

Paragraph 5. Neither house, during the session of the Legislature, shall, without the consent of the other, adjourn for more than three days, or to any other place than that in which the two houses shall be sitting.

Paragraph 6. All bills and joint resolutions shall be read three times in each house before final passage. No bill or joint resolution shall be read a third time in either house until after the intervention of one full calendar day following the day of the second reading; but if either house shall resolve by vote of three-fourths of all its members, signified by yeas and nays entered on the journal, that a bill or joint resolution is an emergency measure, it may proceed forthwith from second to third reading. No bill or joint resolution shall pass, unless there shall be a majority of all the members of each body personally present and agreeing thereto, and the yeas and nays of the members voting on such final passage shall be entered on the journal.

Paragraph 7. Members of the Senate and General Assembly shall receive annually, during the term for which they shall have been elected and while they shall hold their office, such compensation as shall, from time to time, be fixed by law and no other allowance or emolument, directly or indirectly, for any purpose whatever. The President of the Senate and the Speaker of the General Assembly, each by virtue of his office, shall receive an additional allowance, equal to one-third of his compensation as a member.

Paragraph 8. The compensation of members of the Senate and General Assembly shall be fixed at the first session of the Legislature held after this Constitution takes effect, and may be increased or decreased by law from time to time thereafter, but no increase or decrease shall be effective until the legislative year following the next general election for members of the General Assembly.

Paragraph 9. Members of the Senate and General Assembly shall, in all cases except treason and high misdemeanor, be privileged from arrest during their attendance at the sitting of their respective houses, and in going to and returning from the same; and for any statement, speech or debate in either house or at any meeting of a legislative committee, they shall not be questioned in any other place.

Section V.

Paragraph 1. No member of the Senate or General Assembly, during the term for which the member shall have been elected, shall be nominated, elected or appointed to any State civil office or position, of profit, which shall have been created by law, or the emoluments whereof shall have been increased by law, during such term. The provisions of this paragraph shall not prohibit the election of any person as Governor, as Lieutenant Governor, or as a member of the Senate or General Assembly.

Paragraph 2. The Legislature may appoint any commission, committee or other body whose main purpose is to aid or assist it in performing its functions. Members of the Legislature may be appointed to serve on any such body.

Paragraph 3. If any member of the Legislature shall become a member of Congress or shall accept any Federal or State office or position, of profit, his seat shall thereupon become vacant.

Paragraph 4. No member of Congress, no person holding any Federal or State office or position, of profit, and no judge of any court shall be entitled to a seat in the Legislature.

Paragraph 5. Neither the Legislature nor either house thereof shall elect or appoint any executive, administrative or judicial officer except the State Auditor.

Section VI.

Paragraph 1. All bills for raising revenue shall originate in the General Assembly; but the Senate may propose or concur with amendments, as on other bills.

Paragraph 2. The Legislature may enact general laws under which municipalities, other than counties, may adopt zoning ordinances limiting and restricting to specified districts and regulating therein, buildings and structures, according to their construction, and the nature and extent of their use, and the nature and extent of the uses of land, and the exercise of such authority shall be deemed to be within the police power of the State. Such laws shall be subject to repeal or alteration by the Legislature.

Paragraph 3. Any agency or political subdivision of the State or any agency of a political subdivision thereof, which may be empowered to take or otherwise acquire private property for any public highway, parkway, airport, place, improvement, or use, may be authorized by law to take or otherwise acquire a fee simple absolute or any lesser interest, and may be authorized by law to take or otherwise acquire a fee simple absolute in, easements upon, or the benefit of restrictions upon, abutting property to preserve and protect the public highway, parkway, airport, place, improvement, or use; but such taking shall be with just compensation.

Paragraph 4. The Legislature, in order to insure continuity of State, county and local governmental operations in periods of emergency resulting from disasters caused by enemy attack, shall have the power and the immediate and continuing duty by legislation (1) to provide, prior to the occurrence of the emergency, for prompt and temporary succession to the powers and duties of public offices, of whatever nature and whether filled by election or appointment, the incumbents of which may become unavailable for carrying on the powers and duties of such offices, and (2) to adopt such other measures as may be necessary and proper for insuring the continuity of governmental operations. In the exercise of the powers hereby conferred the Legislature shall in all respects conform to the requirements of this Constitution except to the extent that in the judgment of the Legislature to do so would be impracticable or would admit of undue delay.

Section VII.

Paragraph 1. No divorce shall be granted by the Legislature.

Paragraph 2. No gambling of any kind shall be authorized by the Legislature unless the specific kind, restrictions and control thereof have been heretofore submitted to, and authorized by a majority of the votes cast by, the people at a special election or shall hereafter be submitted to, and authorized by a majority of the votes cast thereon by, the legally qualified voters of the State voting at a general election, except that, without any such submission or authorization:

A. It shall be lawful for bona fide veterans, charitable, educational, religious or fraternal organizations, civic and service clubs, senior citizen associations or clubs, volunteer fire companies and first-aid or rescue squads to conduct, under such restrictions and control as shall from time to time be prescribed by the Legislature by law, games of chance of, and restricted to, the selling of rights to participate, the awarding of prizes, in the specific kind of game of chance sometimes known as bingo or lotto, played with cards bearing numbers or other designations, 5 or more in one line, the holder covering numbers as objects, similarly numbered, are drawn from a receptacle and the game being won by the person who first covers a previously designated arrangement of numbers on such a card, when the entire net proceeds of such games of chance are to be devoted to educational, charitable, patriotic, religious or public-spirited uses, and in the case of bona fide veterans' organizations and senior citizen associations or clubs to the support of such organizations, in any municipality, in which a majority of the qualified voters, voting thereon, at a general or special election as the submission thereof shall be prescribed by the Legislature by law, shall authorize the conduct of such games of chance therein;

B. It shall be lawful for the Legislature to authorize, by law, bona fide veterans, charitable, educational, religious or fraternal organizations, civic and service clubs, senior citizen associations or clubs, volunteer fire companies and first-aid or rescue squads to conduct games of chance of, and restricted to, the selling of rights to participate, and the awarding of prizes, in the specific kinds of games of chance sometimes known as raffles, conducted by the drawing for prizes or by the allotment of prizes by chance, when the entire net proceeds of such games of chance are to be devoted to educational, charitable, patriotic, religious or public-spirited uses, and in the case of bona fide veterans' organizations and senior citizen associations or clubs to the support of such organizations, in any municipality, in which such law shall be adopted by a majority of the qualified voters, voting thereon, at a general or special election as the submission thereof shall be prescribed by law and for the Legislature, from time to time, to restrict and control, by law, the conduct of such games of chance;

C. It shall be lawful for the Legislature to authorize the conduct of State lotteries restricted to the selling of rights to participate therein and the awarding of prizes by drawings when the entire net proceeds of any such lottery shall be for State institutions and State aid for education; provided, however, that it shall not be competent for the Legislature to borrow, appropriate or use, under any pretense whatsoever, lottery net proceeds for the confinement, housing, supervision or treatment of, or education programs for, adult criminal offenders or juveniles adjudged delinquent or for the construction, staffing, support, maintenance or operation of an adult or juvenile correctional facility or institution;

D. It shall be lawful for the Legislature to authorize by law the establishment and operation, under regulation and control by the State, of gambling houses or casinos within the boundaries, as heretofore established, of the city of Atlantic City, county of Atlantic, and to license and tax such operations and equipment used in connection therewith. Any law authorizing the establishment and operation of such gambling establishments shall provide for the State revenues derived therefrom to be applied solely for the purpose of providing funding for reductions in property taxes, rental, telephone, gas, electric, and municipal utilities charges of eligible senior citizens and disabled residents of the State, and for additional or expanded health services or benefits or transportation services or benefits to eligible senior citizens and disabled residents, in accordance with such formulae as the Legislature shall by law provide. The type and number of such casinos or gambling houses and of the gambling games which may be conducted in any such establishment shall be determined by or pursuant to the terms of the law authorizing the establishment and operation thereof.
It shall also be lawful for the Legislature to authorize by law wagering at casinos or gambling houses in Atlantic City on the

results of any professional, college, or amateur sport or athletic event, except that wagering shall not be permitted on a college sport or athletic event that takes place in New Jersey or on a sport or athletic event in which any New Jersey college team participates regardless of where the event takes place;

E. It shall be lawful for the Legislature to authorize, by law, (1) the simultaneous transmission by picture of running and harness horse races conducted at racetracks located within or outside of this State, or both, to gambling houses or casinos in the city of Atlantic City and (2) the specific kind, restrictions and control of wagering at those gambling establishments on the results of those races. The State's share of revenues derived therefrom shall be applied for services to benefit eligible senior citizens as shall be provided by law; and

F. It shall be lawful for the Legislature to authorize, by law, the specific kind, restrictions and control of wagering on the results of live or simulcast running and harness horse races conducted within or outside of this State. The State's share of revenues derived therefrom shall be used for such purposes as shall be provided by law.
It shall also be lawful for the Legislature to authorize by law wagering at current or former running and harness horse racetracks in this State on the results of any professional, college, or amateur sport or athletic event, except that wagering shall not be permitted on a college sport or athletic event that takes place in New Jersey or on a sport or athletic event in which any New Jersey college team participates regardless of where the event takes place.

Paragraph 3. The Legislature shall not pass any bill of attainder, ex post facto law, or law impairing the obligation of contracts, or depriving a party of any remedy for enforcing a contract which existed when the contract was made.

Paragraph 4. To avoid improper influences which may result from intermixing in one and the same act such things as have no proper relation to each other, every law shall embrace but one object, and that shall be expressed in the title. This paragraph shall not invalidate any law adopting or enacting a compilation, consolidation, revision, or rearrangement of all or parts of the statutory law.

Paragraph 5. No law shall be revived or amended by reference to its title only, but the act revived, or the section or sections amended, shall be inserted at length. No act shall be passed which shall provide that any existing law, or any part thereof, shall be made or deemed a part of the act or which shall enact that any existing law, or any part thereof, shall be applicable, except by inserting it in such act.

Paragraph 6. The laws of this State shall begin in the following style: "Be it enacted by the Senate and General Assembly of the State of New Jersey."

Paragraph 7. No general law shall embrace any provision of a private, special or local character.

Paragraph 8. No private, special or local law shall be passed unless public notice of the intention to apply therefore, and of the general object thereof, shall have been previously given. Such notice shall be given at such time and in such manner and shall be so evidenced and the evidence thereof shall be so preserved as may be provided by law.

Paragraph 9. The Legislature shall not pass any private, special or local laws:

(1) Authorizing the sale of any lands belonging in whole or in part to a minor or minors or other persons who may at the time be under any legal disability to act for themselves.

(2) Changing the law of descent.

(3) Providing for change of venue in civil or criminal causes.

(4) Selecting, drawing, summoning or empaneling grand or petit jurors.

(5) Creating, increasing or decreasing the emoluments, term or tenure rights of any public officers or employees.

(6) Relating to taxation or exemption therefrom.

(7) Providing for the management and control of free public schools.

(8) Granting to any corporation, association or individual any exclusive privilege, immunity or franchise whatever.

(9) Granting to any corporation, association or individual the right to lay down railroad tracks.

(10) Laying out, opening, altering, constructing, maintaining and repairing roads or highways.

(11) Vacating any road, town plot, street, alley or public grounds.

(12) Appointing local officers or commissions to regulate municipal affairs.

(13) Regulating the internal affairs of municipalities formed for local government and counties, except as otherwise in this Constitution provided.

The Legislature shall pass general laws providing for the cases enumerated in this paragraph, and for all other cases which, in its judgment, may be provided for by general laws. The Legislature shall pass no special act conferring corporate powers, but shall pass general laws under which corporations may be organized and corporate powers of every nature obtained, subject, nevertheless, to repeal or alteration at the will of the Legislature.

Paragraph 10. Upon petition by the governing body of any municipal corporation formed for local government, or of any county, and by vote of two-thirds of all the members of each house, the Legislature may pass private, special or local laws regulating the internal affairs of the municipality or county. The petition shall be authorized in a manner to be prescribed by general law and shall specify the general nature of the law sought to be passed. Such law shall become operative only if it is adopted by ordinance of the governing body of the municipality or county or by vote of the legally qualified voters thereof. The Legislature shall prescribe in such law or by general law the method of adopting such law, and the manner in which the ordinance of adoption may be enacted or the vote taken, as the case may be.

Paragraph 11. The provisions of this Constitution and of any law concerning municipal corporations formed for local government, or concerning counties, shall be liberally construed in their favor. The powers of counties and such municipal corporations shall include not only those granted in express terms but also those of necessary or fair implication, or incident to the powers expressly conferred, or essential thereto, and not inconsistent with or prohibited by this Constitution or by law.

Paragraph 12. Notwithstanding any other provision of this Constitution and irrespective of any right or interest in maintaining confidentiality, it shall be lawful for the Legislature to authorize by law the disclosure to the general public of information pertaining to the identity, specific and general whereabouts, physical characteristics and criminal history of persons found to have committed a sex offense. The scope, manner and format of the disclosure of such information shall be determined by or pursuant to the terms of the law authorizing the disclosure.

Section VIII.

Paragraph 1. Members of the Legislature shall, before they enter on the duties of their respective offices, take and subscribe the following oath or affirmation: "I do solemnly swear (or affirm) that I will support the Constitution of the United States and the Constitution of the State of New Jersey, and that I will faithfully discharge the duties of Senator (or member of the General Assembly) according to the best of my ability." Members-elect of the Senate or General Assembly are empowered to administer said oath or affirmation to each other.

Paragraph 2. Every officer of the Legislature shall, before he enters upon his duties, take and subscribe the following oath or affirmation: "I do solemnly promise and swear (or affirm) that I will faithfully, impartially and justly perform all the duties of the office of ...., to the best of my ability and understanding; that I will carefully preserve all records, papers, writings, or property entrusted to me for safekeeping by virtue of my office, and make such disposition of the same as may be required by law."

ARTICLE V: EXECUTIVE

Section I.

Paragraph 1. The executive power shall be vested in a Governor.

Paragraph 2. The Governor shall be not less than thirty years of age, and shall have been for at least twenty years a citizen of the United States, and a resident of this State seven years next before election, unless the Governor shall have been absent during that time on the public business of the United States or of this State. A person shall be eligible for the office of Lieutenant Governor only if eligible under this Constitution for the office of Governor.

Paragraph 3. No member of Congress or person holding any office or position, of profit, under this State or the United States shall be Governor or Lieutenant Governor. If the Governor or Lieutenant Governor or person administering the office of Governor shall accept any other office or position, of profit, under this State or the United States, the office of Governor or Lieutenant Governor, as the case may be, shall thereby be vacated. No Governor or Lieutenant Governor shall be elected by the Legislature to any office during the term for which the person shall have been elected Governor or Lieutenant Governor. Article V, Section I, paragraph 3 amended effective January 17, 2006.

Paragraph 4. The Governor and Lieutenant Governor shall be elected conjointly and for concurrent terms by the legally qualified voters of this State, and the manner of election shall require each voter to cast a single vote for both offices. The candidate of each political party for election to the office of Lieutenant Governor shall be selected by the candidate of that party nominated for election to the office of Governor. The selection of the candidate for election to the office of Lieutenant Governor shall be made within 30 days following the nomination of the candidate for election to the office of Governor. A person shall not seek election to both offices simultaneously. The joint candidates receiving the greatest number of votes shall be elected; but if two or more joint candidacies shall be equal and greatest in votes, one set of joint candidates shall be elected by the vote of a majority of all the members of both houses in joint meeting at the regular legislative session next following the election for Governor and Lieutenant Governor by the people. Contested elections for the offices of Governor and Lieutenant Governor shall be determined in such manner as may be provided by law.

Paragraph 5. The term of office of the Governor and of the Lieutenant Governor shall be four years, beginning at noon of the third Tuesday in January next following their election, and ending at noon of the third Tuesday in January four years thereafter. No person who has been elected Governor for two successive terms, including an unexpired term, shall again be eligible for that office until the third Tuesday in January of the fourth year following the expiration of the second successive term.

Paragraph 6. In the event of a vacancy in the office of Governor resulting from the death, resignation or removal of a Governor in office, or the death of a Governor-elect, or from any other cause, the Lieutenant Governor shall become Governor, until a new Governor is elected and qualifies.

In the event of simultaneous vacancies in both the offices of Governor and Lieutenant Governor resulting from any cause, the President of the Senate shall become Governor until a new Governor or Lieutenant Governor is elected and qualifies. In the event that there is a vacancy in the office of Senate President, or the Senate President declines to become Governor, then the Speaker of the General Assembly shall become Governor until a new Governor or Lieutenant Governor is elected and qualifies. In the event that there is a vacancy in the office of Speaker of the General Assembly, or if the Speaker declines to become

Governor, then the functions, powers, duties and emoluments of the office shall devolve for the time being upon such officers and in the order of succession as may be provided by law, until a new Governor or Lieutenant Governor is elected and qualifies.

Paragraph 7. In the event of the failure of the Governor-elect to qualify, or of the absence from the State of a Governor in office, or the Governor's inability to discharge the duties of the office, or the Governor's impeachment, the functions, powers, duties and emoluments of the office shall devolve upon the Lieutenant Governor, until the Governor-elect qualifies, or the Governor in office returns to the State, or is no longer unable to discharge the duties of the office, or is acquitted, as the case may be, or until a new Governor is elected and qualifies. In the event that the Lieutenant Governor in office is absent from the State, or is unable to discharge the duties of the office, or is impeached, or if the Lieutenant Governor-elect fails to qualify, or if there is a vacancy in the office of Lieutenant Governor, the functions, powers, duties, and emoluments of the office of Governor shall devolve upon the President of the Senate. In the event there is a vacancy in the office of the President of the Senate, or of the Senate President's absence from the State, inability to discharge the duties of the office, or impeachment, then such functions, powers, duties, and emoluments shall devolve upon the Speaker of the General Assembly. In the event there is a vacancy in the office of Speaker of the General Assembly, or of the Speaker's absence from the State, inability to discharge the duties of the office, or impeachment, then such functions, powers, duties, and emoluments shall devolve upon such officers and in the order of succession as may be provided by law. The functions, powers, duties, and emoluments of the office of Governor shall devolve upon the President of the Senate, the Speaker of the General Assembly or another officer, as the case may be, until the Governor-elect or Lieutenant Governor-elect qualifies, or the Governor or Lieutenant Governor in office returns to the State, or is no longer unable to discharge the duties of the office, or is acquitted, or until a new Lieutenant Governor is appointed, as the case may be, or a new Governor or

Lieutenant Governor is elected and qualifies.

Paragraph 8. Whenever a Governor-elect or Lieutenant Governor-elect shall have failed to qualify within six months after the beginning of the term of office, or whenever for a period of six months a Governor or Lieutenant Governor in office, or person administering the office, shall have remained continuously absent from the State, or shall have been continuously unable to discharge the duties of the office by reason of mental or physical disability, the office shall be deemed vacant. Such vacancy shall be determined by the Supreme Court upon presentment to it of a concurrent resolution declaring the ground of the vacancy, adopted by a vote of two-thirds of all the members of each house of the Legislature, and upon notice, hearing before the Court and proof of the existence of the vacancy.

Paragraph 9. In the event of a vacancy in the office of Lieutenant Governor resulting from the death, resignation or removal of a Lieutenant Governor in office or the death of a Lieutenant Governor-elect or from any other cause, the Governor shall appoint a Lieutenant Governor within forty-five days of the occurrence of the vacancy to fill the unexpired term.
If a Lieutenant Governor becomes Governor, or in the event of simultaneous vacancies in the offices of Governor and Lieutenant Governor, a Governor and a Lieutenant Governor shall be elected to fill the unexpired terms of both offices at the next general election, unless the assumption of the office of Governor by the Lieutenant Governor, or the vacancies, as the case may be, occur within sixty days immediately preceding a general election, in which case they shall be elected at the second succeeding general election. No election to fill the unexpired terms shall be held in any year in which a Governor and Lieutenant Governor are to be elected for full terms. A Governor and Lieutenant Governor elected for unexpired terms shall assume their offices immediately upon their election. Article V, Section I, paragraph 9 amended effective January 17, 2006.

Paragraph 10. a. The Governor and the Lieutenant Governor shall each receive for services a salary, which shall be neither increased nor diminished during the period for which the Governor or Lieutenant Governor shall have been elected or appointed. b. The Governor shall appoint the Lieutenant Governor to serve as the head of a principal department or other executive or administrative agency of State government, or delegate to the Lieutenant Governor duties of the office of Governor, or both. The Governor shall not appoint the Lieutenant Governor to serve as Attorney General. The Lieutenant Governor shall in addition perform such other duties as may be provided by law.

Paragraph 11. The Governor shall take care that the laws be faithfully executed. To this end he shall have power, by appropriate action or proceeding in the courts brought in the name of the State, to enforce compliance with any constitutional or legislative mandate, or to restrain violation of any constitutional or legislative power or duty, by any officer, department or agency of the State; but this power shall not be construed to authorize any action or proceeding against the Legislature.

Paragraph 12. The Governor shall communicate to the Legislature, by message at the opening of each regular session and at such other times as he may deem necessary, the condition of the State, and shall in like manner recommend such measures as he may deem desirable. He may convene the Legislature, or the Senate alone, whenever in his opinion the public interest shall require. He shall be the Commander-in-Chief of all the military and naval forces of the State. He shall grant commissions to all officers elected or appointed pursuant to this Constitution. He shall nominate and appoint, with the advice and consent of the Senate, all officers for whose election or appointment provision is not otherwise made by this Constitution or by law.

Paragraph 13. The Governor may fill any vacancy occurring in any office during a recess of the Legislature, appointment to which may be made by the Governor with the advice and consent of the Senate, or by the Legislature in joint meeting. An ad interim appointment so made shall expire at the end of the next regular session of the Senate, unless a successor shall be sooner appointed and qualify; and after the end of the session no ad interim appointment to the same office shall be made unless the Governor shall have submitted to the Senate a nomination to the office during the session and the Senate shall have adjourned without confirming or rejecting it. No person nominated for any office shall be eligible for an ad interim appointment to such office if the nomination shall have failed of confirmation by the Senate.

Paragraph 14.

(a) When a bill has finally passed both houses, the house in which final action was taken to complete its passage shall cause it to be presented to the Governor before the close of the calendar day next following the date of the session at which such final action was taken.

(b) A passed bill presented to the Governor shall become law:

(1) if the Governor approves and signs it within the period allowed for his consideration; or,

(2) if the Governor does not return it to the house of origin, with a statement of his objections, before the expiration of the period allowed for his consideration; or,

(3) if, upon reconsideration of a bill objected to by the Governor, two-thirds of all the members of each house agree to pass the bill.

(c) The period allowed for the Governor's consideration of a passed bill shall be from the date of presentation until noon of the forty-fifth day next following or, if the house of origin be in temporary adjournment on that day, the first day subsequent upon which the house reconvenes; except that:

(1) if on the said forty-fifth day the Legislature is in adjournment sine die, any bill then pending the Governor's approval shall be returned, if he objects to it, at a special session held pursuant to subparagraph (d) of this paragraph;

(2) any bill passed between the forty-fifth day and the tenth day preceding the expiration of the second legislative year shall be returned by the Governor, if he objects to it, not later than noon of the day next preceding the expiration of the second legislative year;

(3) any bill passed within 10 days preceding the expiration of the second legislative year shall become law only if the Governor signs it prior to noon of the seventh day following such expiration, or the Governor returns it to the House of origin, with a statement of his objections, and two-thirds of all members of each House agree to pass the bill prior to such expiration.

(d) For the purpose of permitting the return of bills pursuant to this paragraph, a special session of the Legislature shall convene, without petition or call, for the sole purpose of acting upon bills returned by the Governor, on the forty-fifth day next following adjournment sine die of the regular session; or, if the second legislative year of a 2-year Legislature will expire before said forty-fifth day, then the day next preceding the expiration of the legislative year.

(e) Upon receiving from the Governor a bill returned by him with his objections, the house in which it originated shall enter the objections at large in its journal or minutes and proceed to reconsider it. If, upon reconsideration, on or after the third day following its return, or the first day of a special session convened for the sole purpose of acting on such bills, two-thirds of all the members of the house of origin agree to pass the bill, it shall be sent, together with the objections of the Governor, to the other house; and if, upon reconsideration, it is approved by two-thirds of all the members of the house, it shall become a law. In all such cases the votes of each house shall be determined by yeas and nays, and the names of the persons voting for and against the bill shall be entered on the journal or minutes of each house.

(f) The Governor, in returning with his objections a bill for reconsideration at any general or special session of the Legislature, may recommend that an amendment or amendments specified by him be made in the bill, and in such case the Legislature may amend and reenact the bill. If a bill be so amended and reenacted, it shall be presented again to the Governor, but shall become a law only if he shall sign it within 10 days after presentation, except that any bill amended and reenacted within 10 days preceding the expiration of the second legislative year shall become law only if the Governor signs it prior to noon of the seventh day following such expiration. No bill shall be returned by the Governor a second time. No bill need be read three times and no emergency resolution need be adopted for the reenactment of any bill at a special session of the Legislature.

Paragraph 15. If any bill presented to the Governor shall contain one or more items of appropriation of money, he may object in whole or in part to any such item or items while approving the other portions of the bill. In such case he shall append to the bill, at the time of signing it, a statement of each item or part thereof to which he objects, and each item or part so objected to shall not take effect. A copy of such statement shall be transmitted by him to the house in which the bill originated, and each item or part thereof objected to shall be separately reconsidered. If upon reconsideration, on or after the third day following said transmittal, one or more of such items or parts thereof be approved by two-thirds of all the members of each house, the same shall become a part of the law, notwithstanding the objections of the Governor. All the provisions of the preceding paragraph in relation to bills not approved by the Governor shall apply to cases in which he shall withhold his approval from any item or items or parts thereof contained in a bill appropriating money.

Section II.

Paragraph 1. The Governor may grant pardons and reprieves in all cases other than impeachment and treason, and may suspend and remit fines and forfeitures. A commission or other body may be established by law to aid and advise the Governor in the exercise of executive clemency.

Paragraph 2. A system for the granting of parole shall be provided by law.

Section III.

Paragraph 1. Provision for organizing, inducting, training, arming, disciplining and regulating a militia shall be made by law, which shall conform to applicable standards established for the armed forces of the United States.

Paragraph 2. The Governor shall nominate and appoint all general and flag officers of the militia, with the advice and consent of the Senate. All other commissioned officers of the militia shall be appointed and commissioned by the Governor according to law.

Section IV.

Paragraph 1. All executive and administrative offices, departments, and instrumentalities of the State government, including the offices of Secretary of State and Attorney General, and their respective functions, powers and duties, shall be allocated by law among and within not more than twenty principal departments, in such manner as to group the same according to major purposes so far as practicable. Temporary commissions for special purposes may, however, be established by law and such commissions need not be allocated within a principal department.

Paragraph 2. Each principal department shall be under the supervision of the Governor. The head of each principal department shall be a single executive unless otherwise provided by law. Such single executives shall be nominated and appointed by the Governor, with the advice and consent of the Senate, to serve at the pleasure of the Governor during the Governor's term of office and until the appointment and qualification of their successors, except as herein otherwise provided with respect to the Secretary of State and the Attorney General. The Governor may appoint the Lieutenant Governor to serve as the head of a principal department, without the advice and consent of the Senate, and to serve at the pleasure of the Governor during the Governor's term of office.

Paragraph 3. The Secretary of State and the Attorney General shall be nominated and appointed by the Governor with the advice and consent of the Senate to serve during the term of office of the Governor, except the Governor may appoint the Lieutenant Governor to serve as Secretary of State without the advice and consent of the Senate.

Paragraph 4. Whenever a board, commission or other body shall be the head of a principal department, the members thereof shall be nominated and appointed by the Governor with the advice and consent of the Senate, and may be removed in the manner provided by law. The Governor may appoint the Lieutenant Governor hereto without the advice and consent of the Senate. Such a board, commission or other body may appoint a principal executive officer when authorized by law, but the appointment shall be subject to the approval of the Governor. Any principal executive officer so appointed shall be removable by the Governor, upon notice and an opportunity to be heard.

Paragraph 5. The Governor may cause an investigation to be made of the conduct in office of any officer or employee who receives his compensation from the State of New Jersey, except a member, officer or employee of the Legislature or an officer elected by the Senate and General Assembly in joint meeting, or a judicial officer. He may require such officers or employees to submit to him a written statement or statements, under oath, of such information as he may call for relating to the conduct of their respective offices or employments. After notice, the service of charges and an opportunity to be heard at public hearing the Governor may remove any such officer or employee for cause. Such officer or employee shall have the right of judicial review, on both the law and the facts, in such manner as shall be provided by law.

Paragraph 6. No rule or regulation made by any department, officer, agency or authority of this state, except such as relates to the organization or internal management of the State government or a part thereof, shall take effect until it is filed either with the Secretary of State or in such other manner as may be provided by law. The Legislature shall provide for the prompt publication of such rules and regulations. The Legislature may review any rule or regulation to determine if the rule or regulation is consistent with the intent of the Legislature as expressed in the language of the statute which the rule or regulation is intended to implement. Upon a finding that an existing or proposed rule or regulation is not consistent with legislative intent, the Legislature shall transmit this finding in the form of a concurrent resolution to the Governor and the head of the Executive Branch agency which promulgated, or plans to promulgate, the rule or regulation. The agency shall have 30 days to amend or withdraw the existing or proposed rule or regulation. If the agency does not amend or withdraw the existing or proposed rule or regulation, the Legislature may invalidate that rule or regulation, in whole or in part, or may prohibit that proposed rule or regulation, in whole or in part, from taking effect by a vote of a majority of the authorized membership of each House in favor of a concurrent resolution providing for invalidation or prohibition, as the case may be, of the rule or regulation. This vote shall not take place until at least 20 calendar days after the placing on the desks of the members of each House of the Legislature in open meeting of the transcript of a public hearing held by either House on the invalidation or prohibition of the rule or regulation.

ARTICLE VI: JUDICIAL SECTION

Section I.

Paragraph 1. The judicial power shall be vested in a Supreme Court, a Superior Court, and other courts of limited jurisdiction. The other courts and their jurisdiction may from time to time be established, altered or abolished by law.

Section II.

Paragraph 1. The Supreme Court shall consist of a Chief Justice and six Associate Justices. Five members of the court shall constitute a quorum. When necessary, the Chief Justice shall assign the Judge or Judges of the Superior Court, senior in service, as provided by rules of the Supreme Court, to serve temporarily in the Supreme Court. In case the Chief Justice is absent or unable to serve, a presiding Justice designated in accordance with rules of the Supreme Court shall serve temporarily in his stead.

Paragraph 2. The Supreme Court shall exercise appellate jurisdiction in the last resort in all causes provided in this Constitution.
3. The Supreme Court shall make rules governing the administration of all courts in the State and, subject to the law, the practice and procedure in all such courts. The Supreme Court shall have jurisdiction over the admission to the practice of law and the discipline of persons admitted.

Section III.

Paragraph 1. The Superior Court shall consist of such number of judges as may be authorized by law, each of whom shall exercise the powers of the court subject to rules of the Supreme Court. The Superior Court shall at all times consist of at least two judges who shall be assigned to sit in each of the counties of this State, and who are resident therein at the time of appointment and reappointment.

Paragraph 2. The Superior Court shall have original general jurisdiction throughout the State in all causes.

Paragraph 3. The Superior Court shall be divided into an Appellate Division, a Law Division, and a Chancery Division, which shall include a family part. Each division shall have such other parts, consist of such number of judges, and hear such causes, as may be provided by rules of the Supreme Court. At least two judges of the Superior Court shall at all times be assigned to sit in each of the counties of the State, who at the time of their appointment and reappointment were residents of that county provided, however, that the number of judges required to reside in the county wherein they sit shall be at least equal in number to the number of judges of the county court sitting in each of the counties at the adoption of this amendment.

Paragraph 4. Subject to rules of the Supreme Court, the Law Division and the Chancery Division shall each exercise the powers and functions of the other division when the ends of justice so require, and legal and equitable relief shall be granted in any cause so that all matters in controversy between the parties may be completely determined.

Section IV.

Repealed.

Section V.

Paragraph 1. Appeals may be taken to the Supreme Court:

(a) In causes determined by the appellate division of the Superior Court involving a question arising under the Constitution of the United States or this State;

(b) In causes where there is a dissent in the Appellate Division of the Superior Court;

(c) In capital causes;

(d) On certification by the Supreme Court to the Superior Court and, where provided by rules of the Supreme Court, to the inferior courts; and

(e) In such causes as may be provided by law.

Paragraph 2. Appeals may be taken to the Appellate Division of the Superior Court from the law and chancery divisions of the Superior Court and in such other causes as may be provided by law.

Paragraph 3. The Supreme Court and the Appellate Division of the Superior Court may exercise such original jurisdiction as may be necessary to the complete determination of any cause on review.

Paragraph 4. Prerogative writs are superseded and, in lieu thereof, review, hearing and relief shall be afforded in the Superior Court, on terms and in the manner provided by rules of the Supreme Court, as of right, except in criminal causes where such review shall be discretionary.

Section VI.

Paragraph 1. The Governor shall nominate and appoint, with the advice and consent of the Senate, the Chief Justice and associate justices of the Supreme Court, the Judges of the Superior Court, and the judges of the inferior courts with jurisdiction extending to more than one municipality; except that upon the abolition of the juvenile and domestic relations courts or family court and county district courts as provided by law, the judges of those former courts shall become the Judges of the Superior Court without nomination by the Governor or confirmation by the Senate. No nomination to such an office shall be sent to the Senate for confirmation until after 7 days' public notice by the Governor.

Paragraph 2. The justices of the Supreme Court and the judges of the Superior Court shall each prior to his appointment have been admitted to the practice of law in this State for at least 10 years.

Paragraph 3. The Justices of the Supreme Court and the Judges of the Superior Court shall hold their offices for initial terms of 7 years and upon reappointment shall hold their offices during good behavior; provided however, that, upon the abolition of the juvenile and domestic relations courts or family court and county district courts as provided by law, the judges in office in those former courts who have acquired tenure and the Judges of the Superior Court who have acquired tenure as a judge in those former courts prior to appointment to the Superior Court, shall have tenure as Judges of the Superior Court. Judges of the juvenile and domestic relations courts or family court and county district courts who have not acquired tenure as a judge of those former courts shall hold their offices for the period of their respective terms which remain unexpired and shall acquire tenure upon reappointment to the Superior Court. Such justices and judges shall be retired upon attaining the age of 70 years. Provisions for the pensioning of the Justices of the Supreme Court and the Judges of the Superior Court shall be made by law.

Paragraph 4. The Justices of the Supreme Court and the Judges of the Superior Court shall be subject to impeachment, and any judicial officer impeached shall not exercise his office until acquitted. The Judges of the Superior Court shall also be subject to removal from office by the Supreme Court for such causes and in such manner as shall be provided by law.

Paragraph 5. Whenever the Supreme Court shall certify to the Governor that it appears that any Justice of the Supreme Court or Judge of the Superior Court is so incapacitated as substantially to prevent him from performing his judicial duties, the Governor shall appoint a commission of three persons to inquire into the circumstances; and, on their recommendation, the Governor may retire the justice or judge from office, on pension as may be provided by law.

Paragraph 6. The Justices of the Supreme Court and the Judges of the Superior Court shall receive for their services such salaries as may be provided by law, which shall not be diminished during the term of their appointment, except for deductions from such salaries for contributions, established by law from time to time, for pensions as provided for under paragraphs 3 and 5 of Section VI of this Article, health benefits, and other, similar benefits. They shall not, while in office, engage in the practice of law or other gainful pursuit.

Paragraph 7. The Justices of the Supreme Court and the Judges of the Superior Court shall hold no other office or position, of profit, under this State or the United States. Any such justice or judge who shall become a candidate for an elective public office shall thereby forfeit his judicial office.[1]

Section VII.

Paragraph 1. The Chief Justice of the Supreme Court shall be the administrative head of all the courts in the State. He shall appoint an Administrative Director to serve at his pleasure.

Paragraph 2. The Chief Justice of the Supreme Court shall assign Judges of the Superior Court to the Divisions and Parts of the Superior Court, and may from time to time transfer Judges from one assignment to another, as need appears. Assignments to the Appellate Division shall be for terms fixed by rules of the Supreme Court.

Paragraph 3. The Clerk of the Supreme Court and the Clerk of the Superior Court shall be appointed by the Supreme Court for such terms and at such compensation as shall be provided by law.

Section VIII.

Paragraph 1.

a. On or before July 1, 1997:

(1) The State shall be required to pay for certain judicial and probation costs;

(2) All judicial employees and probation employees shall be employees of the State; and

(3) Any judicial fees and probation fees collected shall be paid to the State Treasury.

b. As used in this section:

(1) "Judicial facility costs" means any costs borne by the counties prior to July 1, 1993 with regard to the operation and maintenance of facilities used by the courts or judicial employees;

(2) "Probation facility costs" means any costs borne by the counties prior to July 1, 1993 with regard to the operation and maintenance of facilities used by probation employees;

(3) "Judicial costs" means the costs incurred by the county for funding the judicial system, including but not limited to the following costs: salaries, health benefits and pension payments of all judicial employees, juror fees and library material costs ,except that judicial costs shall not include costs incurred by employees of the surrogate's office or judicial facility costs;

(4) "Judicial employees" means any person employed by the county prior to July 1, 1993 to perform judicial functions, including but not limited to employees working for the courts, and the law library and employees of the sheriff's office who act as court aides, except that employees of the surrogate's office and probation employees shall not be construed to be judicial employees;

(5) "Judicial fees" means any fees or fines collected by the judiciary but shall not include sheriff's or surrogate's fees or municipal court fees or fines;

(6) "Judicial functions" means any duties and responsibilities performed in providing any services and direct support necessary for the effective operation of the judicial system;

(7) "Probation costs" means any costs incurred by the county for the operation of the county probation department, including but not limited to the costs of salaries, health benefits, and pension payments of probation employees but shall not include probation facility costs;

(8) "Probation employees" means any person employed by a county probation department prior to July 1,1993;

(9) "Probation fees" means any fees or fines collected in connection with the probation of any persons.

ARTICLE VII: PUBLIC OFFICERS AND EMPLOYEES

Section I.

Paragraph 1. Every State officer, before entering upon the duties of his office, shall take and subscribe an oath or affirmation to support the Constitution of this State and of the United States and to perform the duties of his office faithfully, impartially and justly to the best of his ability.

Paragraph 2. Appointments and promotions in the civil service of the State, and of such political subdivisions as may be provided by law, shall be made according to merit and fitness to be ascertained, as far as practicable, by examination, which, as far as practicable, shall be competitive; except that preference in appointments by reason of active service in any branch of the military or naval forces of the United States in time of war may be provided by law.

Paragraph 3. Any compensation for services or any fees received by any person by virtue of an appointive State office or position, in addition to the annual salary provided for the office or position, shall immediately upon receipt be paid into the treasury of the State, unless the compensation or fees shall be allowed or appropriated to him by law.

Paragraph 4. Any person before or after entering upon the duties of any public office, position or employment in this State may be required to give bond as may be provided by law.

Paragraph 5. The term of office of all officers elected or appointed pursuant to the provisions of this Constitution, except as herein otherwise provided, shall commence on the day of the date of their respective commissions; but no commission for any office shall bear date prior to the expiration of the term of the incumbent of said office.

Paragraph 6. The State Auditor shall be appointed by the Senate and General Assembly in joint meeting for a term of five years and until his successor shall be appointed and qualify. It shall be his duty to conduct post-audits of all transactions and accounts kept by or for all departments, offices and agencies of the State government, to report to the Legislature or to any committee thereof as shall be required by law, and to perform such other similar or related duties as shall, from time to time, be required of him by law.

Section II.

Paragraph 1. County prosecutors shall be nominated and appointed by the Governor with the advice and consent of the Senate. Their term of office shall be five years, and they shall serve until the appointment and qualification of their respective successors.

Paragraph 2. County clerks, surrogates and sheriffs shall be elected by the people of their respective counties at general elections. The term of office of county clerks and surrogates shall be five years, and of sheriffs three years. Whenever a vacancy shall occur in any such office it shall be filled in the manner to be provided by law.

Section III.

Paragraph 1. The Governor and all other State officers, while in office and for two years thereafter, shall be liable to impeachment for misdemeanor committed during their respective continuance in office.

Paragraph 2. The General Assembly shall have the sole power of impeachment by vote of a majority of all the members. All impeachments shall be tried by the Senate, and members, when sitting for that purpose, shall be on oath or affirmation "truly and impartially to try and determine the charge in question according to the evidence". No person shall be convicted without the concurrence of two-thirds of all the members of the Senate. When the Governor is tried, the Chief Justice of the Supreme Court shall preside and the President of the Senate shall not participate in the trial.

Paragraph 3. Judgment in cases of impeachment shall not extend further than to removal from office, and to disqualification to hold and enjoy any public office of honor, profit or trust in this State; but the person convicted shall nevertheless be liable to indictment, trial and punishment according to law.

ARTICLE VIII: TAXATION AND FINANCE

Section I.

Paragraph 1. Property shall be assessed for taxation under general laws and by uniform rules. All real property assessed and taxed locally or by the State for allotment and payment to taxing districts shall be assessed according to the same standard of value; and such real property shall be taxed at the general tax rate of the taxing district in which the property is situated, for the use of such taxing district.

Paragraph 2. Exemption from taxation may be granted only by general laws. Until otherwise provided by law all exemptions from taxation validly granted and now in existence shall be continued. Exemptions from taxation may be altered or repealed, except those exempting real and personal property used exclusively for religious, educational, charitable or cemetery purposes, as defined by law, and owned by any corporation or association organized and conducted exclusively for one or more of such purposes and not operating for profit.

Paragraph 3. Any citizen and resident of this State now or hereafter honorably discharged or released under honorable circumstances from active service in time of war in any branch of the armed forces of the United States, shall be exempt from taxation on real and personal property to an aggregate assessed valuation not exceeding five hundred dollars, which exemption shall not be altered or repealed. Any person hereinabove described who has been or shall be declared by the United States Veterans Administration, or its successor, to have a service-connected disability, shall be entitled to such further exemption from taxation as from time to time may be provided by law. The widow of any citizen and resident of this State who has met or shall meet his death on active duty in time of war in any such service shall be entitled, during her widowhood, to the exemption in this paragraph provided for honorably discharged veterans and to such further exemption as from time to time may be provided by law.

Section II.

Paragraph 1. The credit of the State shall not be directly or indirectly loaned in any case.

Paragraph 2. No money shall be drawn from the State treasury but for appropriations made by law. All moneys for the support of the State government and for all other State purposes as far as can be ascertained or reasonably foreseen, shall be provided for in one general appropriation law covering one and the same fiscal year; except that when a change in the fiscal year is made, necessary provision may be made to effect the transition. No general appropriation law or other law appropriating money for any State purpose shall be enacted if the appropriation contained therein, together with all prior appropriations made for the same fiscal period, shall exceed the total amount of revenue on hand and anticipated which will be available to meet such appropriations during such fiscal period, as certified by the Governor.

Paragraph 3. The Legislature shall not, in any manner, create in any fiscal year a debt or debts, liability or liabilities of the State, which together with any previous debts or liabilities shall exceed at any time one per centum of the total amount appropriated by the general appropriation law for that fiscal year, unless the same shall be authorized by a law for some single object or work distinctly specified therein. Regardless of any limitation relating to taxation in this Constitution, such law shall provide the ways and means, exclusive of loans, to pay the interest of such debt or liability as it falls due, and also to pay and discharge the principal thereof within thirty-five years from the time it is contracted; and the law shall not be repealed until such debt or liability and the interest thereon are fully paid and discharged. No such law shall take effect until it shall have been submitted to the people at a general election and approved by a majority of the legally qualified voters of the State voting thereon. All money to be raised by the authority of such law shall be applied only to the specific object stated therein, and to the payment of the debt thereby created. This paragraph shall not be construed to refer to any money that has been or may be deposited with this State by the government of the United States. Nor shall anything in this paragraph contained apply to the creation of any debts or liabilities for purposes of war, or to repel invasion, or to suppress insurrection or to meet an emergency caused by disaster or act of God.

Section III.

Paragraph 1. The clearance, replanning, development or redevelopment of blighted areas shall be a public purpose and public use, for which private property may be taken or acquired. Municipal, public or private corporations may be authorized by law to undertake such clearance, replanning, development or redevelopment; and improvements made for these purposes and uses, or for any of them, may be exempted from taxation, in whole or in part, for a limited period of time during which the profits of and dividends payable by any private corporation enjoying such tax exemption shall be limited by law. The conditions of use, ownership, management and control of such improvements shall be regulated by law.

Paragraph 2. No county, city, borough, town, township or village shall hereafter give any money or property, or loan its money or credit, to or in aid of any individual, association or corporation, or become security for, or be directly or indirectly the owner of, any stock or bonds of any association or corporation.

Paragraph 3. No donation of land or appropriation of money shall be made by the State or any county or municipal corporation to or for the use of any society, association or corporation whatever.

Section IV.

Paragraph 1. The Legislature shall provide for the maintenance and support of a thorough and efficient system of free public schools for the instruction of all the children in the State between the ages of five and eighteen years.

Paragraph 2. The fund for the support of free public schools, and all money, stock and other property, which may hereafter be appropriated for that purpose, or received into the treasury under the provision of any law heretofore passed to augment the said fund, shall be securely invested, and remain a perpetual fund; and the income thereof, except so much as it may be judged expedient to apply to an increase of the capital, shall be annually appropriated to the support of free public schools, for the equal benefit of all the people of the State; and it shall not be competent for the Legislature to borrow, appropriate or use the said fund or any part thereof for any other purpose, under any pretense whatever.

Paragraph 3. The Legislature may, within reasonable limitations as to distance to be prescribed, provide for the transportation of children within the ages of five to eighteen years inclusive to and from any school.

ARTICLE IX: AMENDMENTS

Paragraph 1. Any specific amendment or amendments to this Constitution may be proposed in the Senate or General Assembly. At least twenty calendar days prior to the first vote thereon in the house in which such amendment or amendments are first introduced, the same shall be printed and placed on the desks of the members of each house. Thereafter and prior to such vote a public hearing shall be held thereon. If the proposed amendment or amendments or any of them shall be agreed to by three-fifths of all the members of each of the respective houses, the same shall be submitted to the people. If the same or any of them shall be agreed to by less then three-fifths but nevertheless by a majority of all the members of each of the respective houses, such proposed amendment or amendments shall be referred to the Legislature in the next legislative year; and if in that year the same or any of them shall be agreed to by a majority of all the members of each of the respective houses, then such amendment or amendments shall be submitted to the people.

Paragraph 2. The proposed amendment or amendments shall be entered on the journal of each house with the yeas and nays of the members voting thereon.

Paragraph 3. The Legislature shall cause the proposed amendment or amendments to be published at least once in one or more newspapers of each county, if any be published therein, not less than three months prior to submission to the people.

Paragraph 4. The proposed amendment or amendments shall then be submitted to the people at the next general election in the manner and form provided by the Legislature.

Paragraph 5. If more than one amendment be submitted, they shall be submitted in such manner and form that the people may vote for or against each amendment separately and distinctly.

Paragraph 6. If the proposed amendment or amendments or any of them shall be approved by a majority of the legally qualified voters of the State voting thereon, the same shall become part of the Constitution on the thirtieth day after the election, unless otherwise provided in the amendment or amendments.

Paragraph 7. If at the election a proposed amendment shall not be approved, neither such proposed amendment nor one to effect the same or substantially the same change in the Constitution shall be submitted to the people before the third general election thereafter.

ARTICLE X: GENERAL PROVISIONS

Paragraph 1. The seal of the State shall be kept by the Governor, or person administering the office of Governor, and used by him officially, and shall be called the Great Seal of the State of New Jersey.

Paragraph 2. All grants and commissions shall be in the name and by the authority of the State of New Jersey, sealed with the Great Seal, signed by the Governor, or person administering the office of Governor, and countersigned by the Secretary of State, and shall run thus: "The State of New Jersey, to.............., Greeting".

Paragraph 3. All writs shall be in the name of the State. All indictments shall conclude: "against the peace of this State, the government and dignity of the same".

Paragraph 4. Wherever in this Constitution the term "person", "persons", "people" or any personal pronoun is used, the same shall be taken to include both sexes.

Paragraph 5. Except as herein otherwise provided, this Constitution shall take effect on the first day of January in the year of our Lord one thousand nine hundred and forty-eight.

ARTICLE XI: SCHEDULE

Section I.

Paragraph 1. This Constitution shall supersede the Constitution of one thousand eight hundred and forty-four as amended.

Paragraph 2. The Legislature shall enact all laws necessary to make this Constitution fully effective.

Paragraph 3. All law, statutory and otherwise, all rules and regulations of administrative bodies and all rules of courts in force at the time this Constitution or any Article thereof takes effect shall remain in full force until they expire or are superseded, altered or repealed by this Constitution or otherwise.

Paragraph 4. Except as otherwise provided by this Constitution, all writs, actions, judgments, decrees, causes of action, prosecutions, contracts, claims and rights of individuals and of bodies corporate, and of the State, and all charters and franchises shall continue unaffected notwithstanding the taking effect of any Article of this Constitution.

Paragraph 5. All indictments found before the taking effect of this Constitution or any Article may be proceeded upon. After the taking effect thereof, indictments for crime and complaints for offenses committed prior thereto may be found, made and proceeded upon in the courts having jurisdiction thereof.

Section II.

Paragraph 1. The first Legislature under this Constitution shall meet on the second Tuesday in January, in the year one thousand nine hundred and forty-eight.
2. Each member of the General Assembly, elected at the election in the year one thousand nine hundred and forty-seven, shall hold office for a term beginning at noon of the second Tuesday in

January in the year one thousand nine hundred and forty-eight and ending at noon of the second Tuesday in January in the year one thousand nine hundred and fifty. Each member of the General Assembly elected thereafter shall hold office for the term provided by this Constitution.

Paragraph 3. Each member of the Senate elected in the years one thousand nine hundred and forty-five and one thousand nine hundred and forty-six shall hold office for the term for which he was elected. Each member of the Senate elected in the year one thousand nine hundred and forty-seven shall hold office for a term of four years beginning at noon of the second Tuesday in January following his election. The seats in the Senate which would have been filled in the years hereinafter designated had this Constitution not been adopted shall be filled by election as follows: of those seats which would have been filled by election in the year one thousand nine hundred and forty-eight, three seats, as chosen by the Senate in the year one thousand nine hundred and forty-eight, shall be filled by election in that year for terms of five years, and three, as so chosen, shall be filled by election in that year for terms of three years, and those seats which would have been filled by election in the year one thousand nine hundred and forty-nine shall be filled by election in that year for terms of four years, so that eleven seats in the Senate shall be filled by election in the year one thousand nine hundred and fifty-one and every fourth year thereafter for terms of four years, and the members of the Senate so elected and their successors shall constitute one class to be elected as prescribed in paragraph 2 of Section II of Article IV of this Constitution, and ten seats shall be filled by election in the year one thousand nine hundred and fifty-three and every fourth year thereafter for terms of four years, and the members of the Senate so elected and their successors shall constitute the other class to be elected as prescribed in said paragraph of this Constitution.

Paragraph 4. The provisions of Paragraph 1 of Section V of Article IV of this Constitution shall not prohibit the nomination, election or appointment of any member of the Senate or General Assembly first organized under this Constitution, to any State civil office or position created by this Constitution or created during his first term as such member.

Section III.

Paragraph 1. A Governor shall be elected for a full term at the general election to be held in the year one thousand nine hundred and forty-nine and every fourth year thereafter.

Paragraph 2. The taking effect of this Constitution or any provision thereof shall not of itself affect the tenure, term, status or compensation of any person then holding any public office, position or employment in this State, except as provided in this Constitution. Unless otherwise specifically provided in this Constitution, all constitutional officers in office at the time of its adoption shall continue to exercise the authority of their respective offices during the term for which they shall have been elected or appointed and until the qualification of their successors respectively. Upon the taking effect of this Constitution all officers of the militia shall retain their commissions subject to the provisions of Article V, Section III

Paragraph 3. The Legislature, in compliance with the provisions of this Constitution, shall prior to the first day of July, one thousand nine hundred and forty-nine, and may from time to time thereafter, allocate by law the executive and administrative offices, departments and instrumentalities of the State government among and within the principal departments. If such allocation shall not have been completed within the time limited, the Governor shall call a special session of the Legislature to which he shall submit a plan or plans for consideration to complete such allocation; and no other matters shall be considered at such session.

Section IV.

Paragraph 1. Subsequent to the adoption of this Constitution the Governor shall nominate and appoint, with the advice and consent of the Senate, a Chief Justice and six Associate Justices of the new Supreme Court from among the persons then being the Chancellor, the Chief Justice and Associate Justices of the old Supreme Court, the Vice Chancellors and Circuit Court Judges. The remaining judicial officers enumerated and such Judges of the Court of Errors and Appeals as have been admitted to the practice of law in this State for at least ten years, and are in office on the adoption of the Constitution, shall constitute the Judges of the Superior Court. The Justices of the new Supreme Court and the Judges of the Superior Court so designated shall hold office each for the period of his term which remains unexpired at the time the Constitution is adopted; and if reappointed he shall hold office during good behavior. No Justice of the new Supreme Court or Judge of the Superior Court shall hold his office after attaining the age of seventy years, except, however, that such Justice or Judge may complete the period of his term which remains unexpired at the time the Constitution is adopted.

Paragraph 2. The Judges of the Courts of Common Pleas shall constitute the Judges of the County Courts, each for the period of his term which remains unexpired at the time the Judicial Article of this Constitution takes effect.

Paragraph 3. The Court of Errors and Appeals, the present Supreme Court, the< Court of Chancery, the Prerogative Court and the Circuit Courts shall be abolished when the Judicial Article of this Constitution takes effect; and all their jurisdiction, functions, powers and duties shall be transferred to and divided between the new Supreme Court and the Superior Court according as jurisdiction is vested in each of them under this Constitution.

Paragraph 4. Except as otherwise provided in this Constitution and until otherwise provided by law, all courts now existing in this State, other than those abolished in paragraph 3 hereof, shall continue as if this Constitution had not been adopted, provided, however, that when the Judicial Article of this Constitution takes effect, the jurisdiction, powers and functions of the Court of Common Pleas, Orphans' Court, Court of Oyer and Terminer, Court of Quarter Sessions and Court of Special Sessions of each county, the judicial officers, clerks and employees thereof, and the causes pending therein and their files, shall be transferred to the County Court of the county. All statutory provisions relating to the county courts aforementioned of each county and to the Judge or Judges thereof shall apply to the new County Court of the county and the Judge or Judges thereof, unless otherwise provided by law. Until otherwise provided by law and except as aforestated, the judicial officers, surrogates and clerks of all courts now existing, other than those abolished in paragraph 3 hereof, and the employees of said officers, clerks, surrogates and courts shall continue in the exercise of their duties, as if this Constitution had not been adopted.

Paragraph 5. The Supreme Court shall make rules governing the administration and practice and procedure of the County Courts; and the Chief Justice of the Supreme Court shall be the administrative head of these courts with power to assign any Judge thereof of any county to sit temporarily in the Superior Court or to sit temporarily without the county in a County Court.

Paragraph 6. The Advisory Masters appointed to hear matrimonial proceedings and in office on the adoption of this Constitution shall, each for the period of his term which remains unexpired at the time the Constitution is adopted, continue so to do as Advisory Masters to the Chancery Division of the Superior Court, unless otherwise provided by law.

Paragraph 7. All Special Masters in Chancery, Masters in Chancery, Supreme Court Commissioners and Supreme Court Examiners shall, until otherwise provided by rules of the Supreme Court, continue respectively as Special Masters, Masters, Commissioners and Examiners of the Superior Court, with appropriate similar functions and powers as if this Constitution had not been adopted.

Paragraph 8. When the Judicial Article of this Constitution takes effect:

(a) All causes and proceedings of whatever character pending in the Court of Errors and Appeals shall be transferred to the new Supreme Court;

(b) All causes and proceedings of whatever character pending on appeal or writ of error in the present Supreme Court and in the Prerogative Court and all pending causes involving the prerogative writs shall be transferred to the Appellate Division of the Superior Court;

(c) All causes and proceedings of whatever character pending in the Supreme Court other than those stated shall be transferred to the Superior Court;

(d) All causes and proceedings of whatever character pending in the Prerogative Court other than those stated shall be transferred to the Chancery Division of the Superior Court;

(e) All causes and proceedings of whatever character pending in all other courts which are abolished shall be transferred to the Superior Court.

For the purposes of this paragraph, paragraph 4 and paragraph 9, a cause shall be deemed to be pending notwithstanding that an adjudication has been entered therein, provided the time limited for review has not expired or the adjudication reserves to any party the right to apply for further relief.

Paragraph 9. The files of all causes pending in the Court of Errors and Appeals shall be delivered to the Clerk of the new Supreme Court; and the files of all causes pending in the present Supreme Court, the Court of Chancery and the Prerogative Court shall be delivered to the Clerk of the Superior Court. All other files, books, papers, records and documents and all property of the Court of Errors and Appeals, the present Supreme Court, the Prerogative Court, the Chancellor and the Court of Chancery, or in their custody, shall be disposed of as shall be provided by law.

Paragraph 10. Upon the taking effect of the Judicial Article of this Constitution, all the functions, powers and duties conferred by statute, rules or otherwise upon the Chancellor, the Ordinary, and the Justices and Judges of the courts abolished by this Constitution, to the extent that such functions, powers and duties are not inconsistent with this Constitution, shall be transferred to and may be exercised by Judges of the Superior Court until otherwise provided by law or rules of the new Supreme Court; excepting that such statutory powers not related to the administration of justice as are then vested in any such judicial officers shall, after the Judicial Article of this Constitution takes effect and until otherwise provided by law, be transferred to and exercised by the Chief Justice of the new Supreme Court.

Paragraph 11. Upon the taking effect of the Judicial Article of this Constitution, the Clerk of the Supreme Court shall become the Clerk of the new Supreme Court and shall serve as such Clerk until the expiration of the term for which he was appointed as Clerk of the Supreme Court, and all employees of the Supreme Court as previously constituted, of the Clerk thereof and of the Chief Justice and the Justices thereof, of the Circuit Courts and the Judges thereof and of the Court of Errors and Appeals shall be transferred to appropriate similar positions with similar compensation and civil service statusunder the Clerk of the new Supreme Court or the new Supreme Court, or the Clerk of the Superior Court or the Superior Court, which shall be provided by law.

Paragraph 12. Upon the taking effect of the Judicial Article of this Constitution, the Clerk in Chancery shall become the Clerk of the Superior Court and shall serve as such Clerk until the expiration of the term for which he was appointed as Clerk in Chancery, and all employees of the Clerk in Chancery, the Court of Chancery, the Chancellor and the several Vice Chancellors shall be transferred to appropriate similar positions with similar compensation and civil service status under the Clerk of the Superior Court or the Superior Court, which shall be provided by law.

Paragraph 13. Appropriations made by law for judicial expenditures during the fiscal year one thousand nine hundred and forty-eight – one thousand nine hundred and forty-nine may be transferred to similar objects and purposes required by the Judicial Article.

Paragraph 14. The Judicial Article of this Constitution shall take effect on the fifteenth day of September, one thousand nine hundred and forty-eight, except that the Governor, with the advice and consent of the Senate, shall have the power to fill vacancies arising prior thereto in the new Supreme Court and the Superior Court; and except further that any provision of this Constitution which may require any act to be done prior thereto or in preparation therefor shall take effect immediately upon the adoption of this Constitution.

Done in Convention, at Rutgers University, the State University of New Jersey, in New Brunswick, on the tenth day of September, in the year of our Lord one thousand nine hundred and forty-seven, and of the independence of the United States of America the one hundred and seventy second.

Robert C. Clothier, President of the Convention

Oliver F. Van Camp, Secretary of the Convention

DELEGATES TO THE CONVENTION

Charles K. Barton
Jane Barus
Franklin H. Berry
Thomas J. Brogan
A.J. Cafiero
Percy Camp
Robert Carey
Dominic A. Cavicchia
Alfred C. Clapp
Robert C. Clothier
Marion Constantine
Joseph W. Cowgill
Allan R. Cullimore
Joseph A. Delaney
Amos F. Dixon
Lester A. Drenk
John Drewen
William A. Dwyer
William J. Dwyer
Frank H. Eggers
Sigurd A. Emerson
Frank S. Farley
Milton A. Feller
Leland F. Ferry
Arthur R. Gemberling
Ronald D. Glass
Myra C. Hacker
William L. Hadley
Lewis G. Hansen
Albert H. Holland
Charles P. Hutchinson
Nathan L. Jacobs
Christian J. Jorgensen
Marie H. Katzenbach
Henry T. Kays
Wesley L. Lance

Leon Leonard
Arthur W. Lewis
Milton C. Lightner
Francis V. D. Lloyd
Thorn Lord
Edward A. McGrath
Wayne D. McMurray
Gene W. Miller
Spencer Miller, Jr.
John Milton
John L. Montgomery
J. Francis Moroney
John L. Morrissey
Francis D. Murphy
Frank J. Murray
George T. Naame
Edward J. O'Mara
William J. Orchard
Lawrence N. Park
Winston Paul
Henry W. Peterson
Pauline H. Peterson
Haydn Proctor
John H. Pursel
H. Rivington Pyne
John J. Rafferty
Oliver Randolph
William T. Read
Olive C. Sanford
Wilbour E. Saunders
John F. Schenk
Frank G. Schlosser
Ralph J. Smalley
George F. Smith
J. Spencer Smith
Frank H. Sommer

Francis A. Stanger, Jr.
Ruth C. Streeter
Clyde W. Struble
Wesley A. Taylor
David Van Alstyne, Jr.

George H. Walton
Elmer H. Wene
Walter G. Winne
David Young, 3rd

www.ingramcontent.com/pod-product-compliance
Lightning Source LLC
Chambersburg PA
CBHW030034230526
45472CB00002B/507